How To Play The Ocarina

A Complete Guide To Learn How To Play Ocarina: Essential Techniques For Beginners

Copyright@2021

Carlo Priore

Table Of Content

CHAPTER ONE

The Ocarina

The ocarina is an uncommon wind instrument manufactured in a variety of shapes as well as sizes. The ocarina and a recorder produce quite related sounds in spite of how different they appear. You might be aware of the ocarina as an instrument through a fandom of Nintendo's Zelda games. However you came to the instrument, the ocarina is an entertaining and simple way to play around with a melody.

Purchasing A Beginner's Ocarina

1- You can shop for your ocarina online.

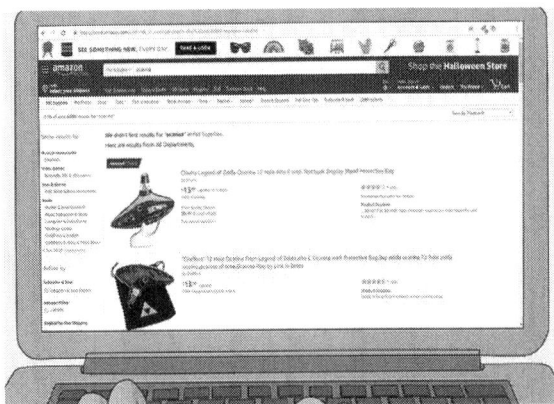

Since it is such an uncommon instrument, you might find it fairly hard-pressed to get one in a music store. With a slight research, you will find scores of online sellers who sell what you are looking for—ranging from Amazon to dealers who specialize in high-quality ocarinas.

- If you are just learning the way to play this instrument, don't break the bank on your first ocarina. $20 to $60 will get you a great starter instrument.
- If you deeply your new hobby and would like to invest in an instrument, super ocarinas can run as high as $500.

2- Choose a pitch range.

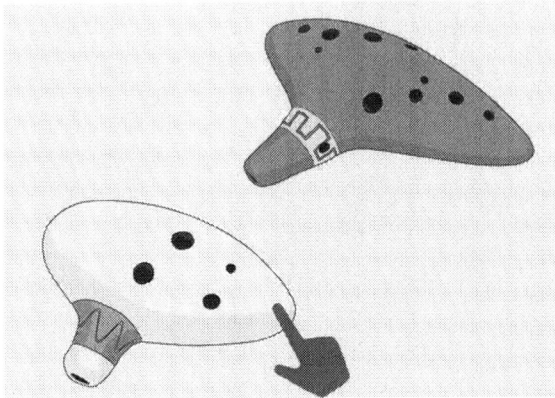

Ocarinas don't cover a broad range of sounds, like a piano does, so it is vital to select an ocarina that is going to play the pitch you desire. In descending order from highest to lowest pitch range, you may well find alto, tenor, soprano, and bass ocarinas.

- The higher the range, the smaller the instrument, thus remember this when selecting your instrument.

3- Select an ocarina style that best suits your skill level.

A four-hole or six-hole ocarina will be the most excellent style to learn on, as they are usually low-cost, light, and effortlessly produce a broad range of notes with very few finger patterns.

- A four-hole ocarina may well produce a fundamental scale of eight notes.
- A six-hole ocarina may well produce a fundamental scale and semitones.

4- Stay away from Peruvian and plastic ocarinas.

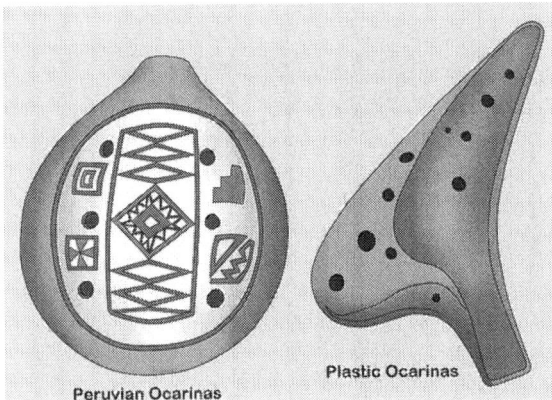

Plastic Ocarinas

Peruvian Ocarinas

Peruvian ocarinas are magnificently styled and comprehensive, so you might be tempted to purchase one on aesthetics alone. Nonetheless, they are typically crafted with inexpensive materials, and don't sound well as a result. They are more attractive than helpful for playing purposes. Plastic ocarinas, though seductively inexpensive, are usually 'airy' and inappropriately tuned.

CHAPTER TWO

Play A Four-Hole Ocarina

1- Look for a user's manual.

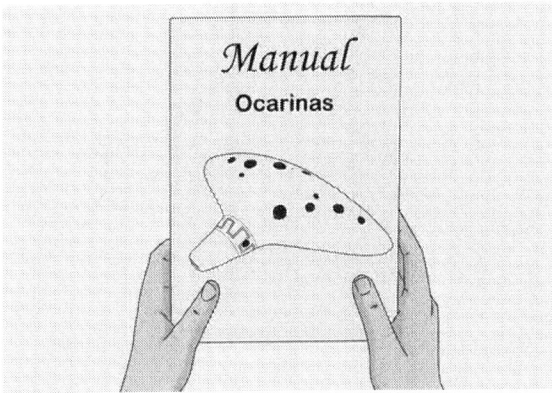

At times, ocarinas come with an instrument chart or other guidelines on the way to play the instrument. If it did, read the chart to observe which holes you have to cover to produce a particular note.

- If your ocarina did not carry a user's manual, follow the guidelines in the next step.

2- Label as well as memorize the holes.

You may well produce a broad range of sounds by covering and uncovering diverse combinations of the four holes with your fingers. As such, you would like to ensure that you have a labeling system that enables you remember which combinations produce particular sounds.

- Place the ocarina's mouthpiece in your mouth as if you wanted to play it and look at the positioning of the holes from this perspective.
- In your head, try to label the top left hole '1', the top right '2', bottom left '3', and the bottom right hole '4.'
- Drill those hole positions into your mind so that you may well learn these guidelines for how to play scales.

- An "x" will be used to be a symbol of an open hole, meaning you must not cover that hole with your finger.

- So, for instance, a Middle C is signified as 1 2 3 4. This implies you must cover all four holes with your pointer as well as middle fingers while blowing all the way through the mouthpiece.

- A D, however, is represented as 1 X 3 4. This implies that all holes must be covered apart from for hole 2 — the top right hole.

3- Study your basic scales.

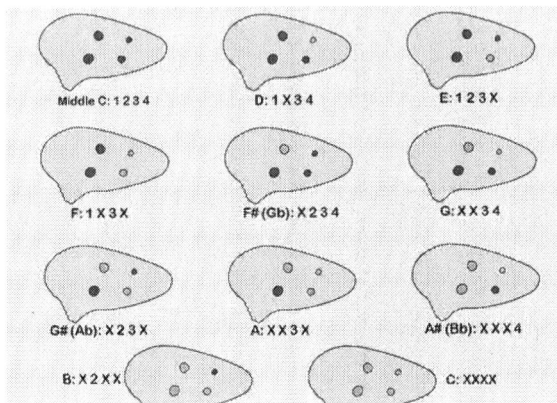

Go through them gradually at first and endeavor to memorize the finger patterns necessary to form this progression of notes. Don't be anxious about speed yet — simply memorize the way to play a scale. Make use of the following finger patterns to work through the scales:

- Middle C: 1 2 3 4

- D: 1 X 3 4
- E: 1 2 3 X
- F: 1 X 3 X
- F# (Gb): X 2 3 4
- G: X X 3 4
- G# (Ab): X 2 3 X
- A: X X 3 X
- A# (Bb): X X X 4
- B: X 2 X X
- C: X X X X

4- Try to practice your scales.

What you can do to become a skillful ocarina player is to acquire the ability to move up and down your scales. There are two things you would like to focus on for the period of this practice: 1) memorizing the notes created by your finger patterns and 2) speed. The more you improve on those two things, the more you will be able to get pleasure from the actual music you are playing.

- A scale of C progresses is therefore: C-D-E-F-G-A-B-C.
- Practice it ascending and descending, that is going up and down. This is the basis for several pieces you will play.

5- Become acquainted with musical notations.

Everybody knows what musical notes resemble, however being able to translate them into an actual song may be past your grasp. Though numerous people take lessons with expert teachers to study musical notations, you can locate several places online where you can learn the techniques to read music without charge. As soon as you can read music, you will be capable to play along with the melodies to your much loved songs with your ocarina.

- You can get sheet music for your much loved songs either by buying books or by searching online.

CHAPTER THREE

Play A Six-Hole Ocarina

1- Look for a user's manual.

Once more, it is always best to check with instructions for a specific instrument instead of general instructions. Learn the chart to see which holes you should cover to produce a particular note.

2- Label as well as memorize the holes.

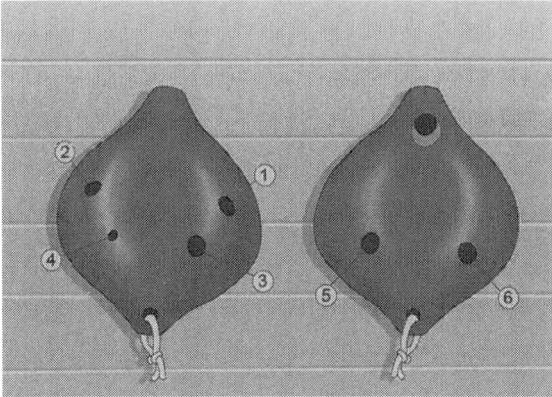

Just like with a four-hole ocarina, the only means you will get some success playing this instrument is by memorizing the technique or way to produce a particular note. You require a labeling system — but this time, for six holes.

- Place the ocarina's mouthpiece in your mouth as if you wanted to play it and look at the positioning of the holes above the instrument from this perspective.
- In your head, label the top left hole '1,' the top right '2,' the bottom left '3,' and the bottom right '4.'
- Afterward envisage the holes on the bottom of the instrument, which may well be covered with your thumbs. You have to label the one on the left '5' and the one on the right '6.'
- Drill those hole positions into your mind so that you may well

can examine these instructions
for how to play scales.

- An 'x' will be utilized to
  represent an open hole,
  implying you must not cover
  that hole with your finger.

3- Practice your fundamental scales.

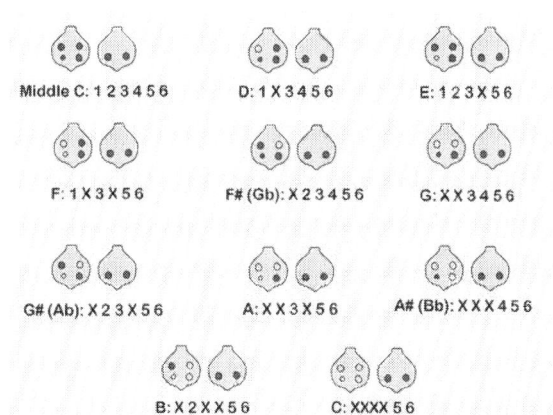

Middle C: 1 2 3 4 5 6   D: 1 X 3 4 5 6   E: 1 2 3 X 5 6

F: 1 X 3 X 5 6   F# (Gb): X 2 3 4 5 6   G: X X 3 4 5 6

G# (Ab): X 2 3 X 5 6   A: X X 3 X 5 6   A# (Bb): X X X 4 5 6

B: X 2 X X 5 6   C: X X X X 5 6

Although the six-hole ocarina has two
additional holes on the back, it utilizes

the same basic system as the four-hole ocarina. The major difference is that to produce the notes from the four-hole instrument, you have to cover the two holes on the bottom even as you follow the same pattern in the top four holes. Commit this scale progression to memory, starting slowly again and concentrating on familiarizing yourself with the notes. Make use of the following finger patterns to work through the scales:

- Middle C: 1 2 3 4 5 6
- D: 1 X 3 4 5 6
- E: 1 2 3 X 5 6
- F: 1 X 3 X 5 6
- F# (Gb): X 2 3 4 5 6

- G: X X 3 4 5 6
- G# (Ab): X 2 3 X 5 6
- A: X X 3 X 5 6
- A# (Bb): X X X 4 5 6
- B: X 2 X X 5 6
- C: XXXX 5 6

4- Learn how to make use of the two bottom holes.

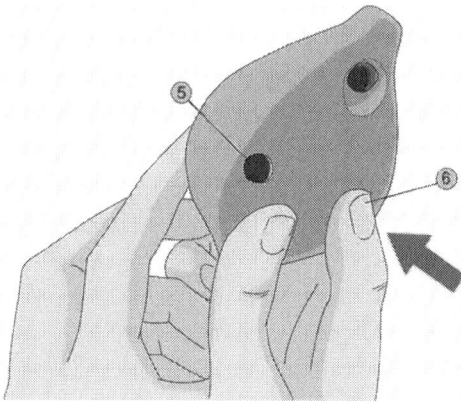

These holes raise the fundamental notes from the preceding step by one step (a semitone) or by two steps (a tone). To raise a note by one step, start with the fingering for the lower note as on a four-hole instrument, however cover hole 5 covered and leave 6 open. To raise a note by two steps, begin once more with the fingering for the lower note on a four-hole instrument, with hole 5 open and 6 covered.

- A semitone moves a note to the next one up in the chromatic scale, eg: C→C#, Ab→A, E→F.
- A tone moves it up two steps in the same scale, eg: C→D, Ab→Bb, E→F#.

- For instance, to play a C#, you would position holes 1-4 for a C (XXXX), then raise one step by uncovering hole 6, so that only hole 5 remains covered: X X X 5 X.
- To effortlessly move from a C to a D without having to move all of your fingers around, you would start with a C (XXXX56) then raise two steps by uncovering hole 5, so that only hole 6 remains covered: X X X X 6.
- This is a quite easier transition for your fingers than XXXX56 to 1X3456.

5- Practicing your scales.

What you can do to become a skillful ocarina player is to be able to move up and down your scales. There are two things you would like to focus on for the period of this practice: 1) memorizing the notes created by your finger patterns and 2) speed. The more you improve on those two things, the more you will be able to get pleasure from the actual music you are playing.

- A scale of C progresses is therefore: C-D-E-F-G-A-B-C.
- Practice it ascending and descending, that is going up and down. This is the basis for several pieces you would play.

6- Become acquainted with musical notations.

Everybody knows what musical notes look like, however being able to translate them into an actual song may be above your grasp. Though several people take lessons with expert teachers to study musical notations, you may well find numerous places online where you can learn how to read music at no cost. As soon as you are able to read music, you can then to play along with the melodies to your much loved songs with your ocarina.

You can locate sheet music for your much loved songs either by buying books or by searching online.

CHAPTER FOUR

Essential Tips

- Try making use of Tablatures, or 'Tabs' to facilitate your learning. They illustrate images of the holes that you should cover in order to play the song.

- If you are purchasing an ocarina to play, don't go for a Peruvian ocarina. Peruvian ocarinas typically say 'handmade in Peru' on the back and are usually un-tuned. The front of Peruvian ocarinas have some kind of painted design, and the quality of the clay used to build them is awful and might make beginners feel unhappy when they hear how their playing sounds. On the other hand, they are grand for collecting.

- Articulate each note by means of saying 'tu' or 'du' at the beginning of each note.

- Begin gradually – you will get pleasure from it more this way, and it will simplicity you into the fundamentals of playing. Do not be over anxious to learn.

- To play high notes, you have to bend your head to obtain better sound.

- Truly practice makes perfect - if you think you actually can't do something, continue trying and shortly it will become easy! Don't get discouraged if you are not getting it at first. You can take a break for a couple of days and resume again.

- Keep your ocarina in a place at approximately room temperature. Excessively high or low temperatures can affect your tuning or even damage or break the wood/plastic.

- Clean the wind way as soon as you finished playing. This is the bit right inside the mouthpiece. To achieve this, find a little strip of newspaper and fold it over itself so it is adequately small to fit through the mouthpiece. You have to slide it inside the ocarina to absorb surplus moisture.

- Brush over the outside of your ocarina using a soft cloth or duster periodically to keep it looking shiny..
- Try not to over blow!

Warnings

- Ocarinas (particularly ceramic) can damage or break easily. Be cautious and keep yours in a case.